t

Lionel

ly

Robo-bot

WHO IS HAPPY?

Billy

Radish
Rabbit

Octo

Joshua

Maisie
Mouse

Good morning, Happyhop House!

Who is **HAPPY** with their new jumper?

Who is **ANGRY** with their friend?

Who is **JEALOUS** of a book?

Everyone is busy getting ready for their day, but how are they all feeling?

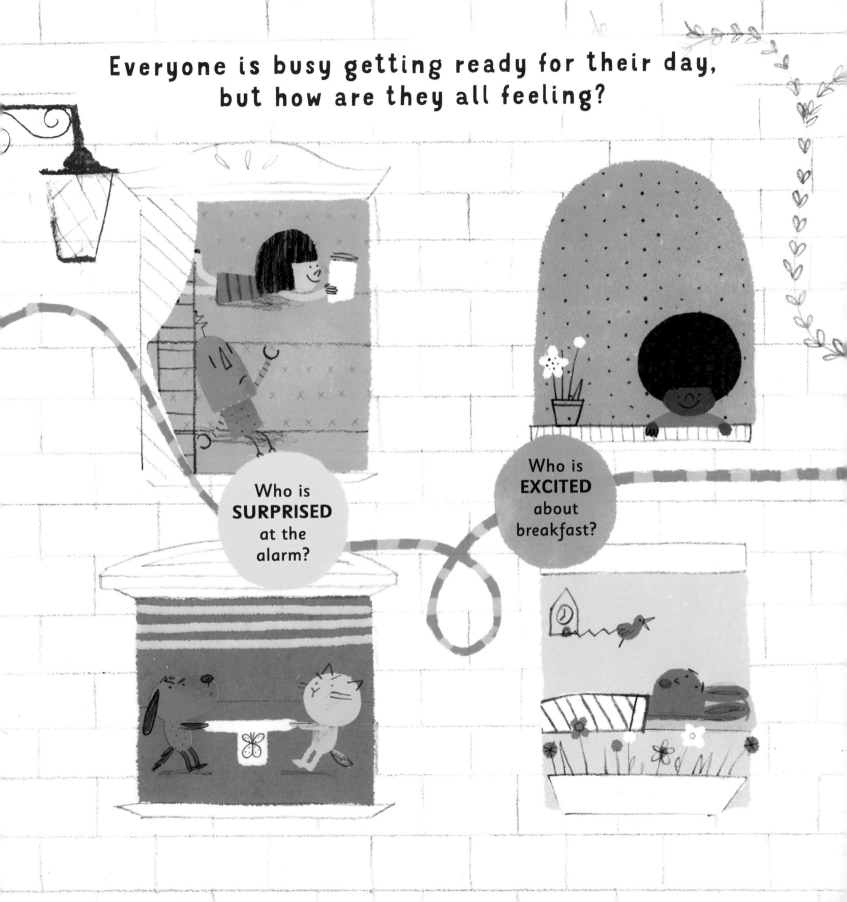

Who is **SURPRISED** at the alarm?

Who is **EXCITED** about breakfast?

Now it's time to go to school.
Hurry! We don't want to be late.

At school, the first lesson the Happyhop Housers have is maths.

Who is **ANGRY** that someone has fallen asleep?

YAWN

Who is **HAPPY** to play paper aeroplanes?

Who is **ANGRY** with their friend?

Now it's time for swimming practice. Watch out, the water's cold!

Who is **ANGRY** with someone for breaking the rules?

NO SPLASHING

Who is **SCARED** to jump off the diving board?

SHIVER BRRR

After all that swimming, everyone's hungry.
Thank goodness it's time for lunch.

Now we're on a school trip at the farm!
Pooooh. It's a bit smelly here.

Who is **WORRIED** about horse-riding?

Who is **SCARED** of the noisy dog?

After school everyone goes to a party.
Can you see who's wearing their birthday crown?

Who is **HAPPY** to have eaten some chocolate cake?

Who is **SAD** that the chocolate cake is gone?

Who has been **SURPRISED** by a balloon popping?

After a very busy day, it's time for the
Happyhop Housers to go home.

How do you feel today?

Angry

You feel angry if you don't get your way, and want to shout and stamp your feet.

Laughing

Laughing is what you do when something is funny! It's a happy feeling.

Excited

You feel excited when you look forward to something fun, like your birthday!

Upset

Upset is when something makes you feel unhappy and angry.

Embarrassed

If you do something silly in front of people, you might feel embarrassed.

Surprised

You feel surprised when you get a shock, or something strange happens.

The people in Happyhop House can feel lots of different things. So can you! Let's learn some more about the feelings in this book.

Sad

Sad is when something happens and you want to cry.

Scared

You can feel scared of things like a monster or the dark.

Worried

You might be worried about a test at school.

Happy

Happy is the good feeling you get when you see a friend.

Jealous

Jealousy is when someone has something you want, like a toy.

Shy

You might feel shy if you meet someone for the first time, and it's a bit scary.

Brimming with creative inspiration, how-to projects, and useful information to enrich your everyday life, Quarto Knows is a favourite destination for those pursuing their interests and passions. Visit our site and dig deeper with our books into your area of interest: Quarto Creates, Quarto Cooks, Quarto Homes, Quarto Lives, Quarto Drives, Quarto Explores, Quarto Gifts, or Quarto Kids.

First published in 2016 by Lincoln Children's Books
This first paperback edition first published in 2019 by Lincoln Children's Books
an imprint of The Quarto Group.
The Old Brewery, 6 Blundell Street, London N7 9BH, United Kingdom.
T (0)20 7700 6700 F (0)20 7700 8066 www.QuartoKnows.com

A catalogue record for this book is available from the British Library.
ISBN 978-1-78603-593-6

Set in Mr Dodo

Published by Rachel Williams
Designed by Andrew Watson and Sasha Moxon
Edited by Katie Cotton
Production by Laura Grandi, Kate O'Riordan and Jenny Cundill
Manufactured in Guangdong, China CC092018
1 3 5 7 9 8 6 4 2